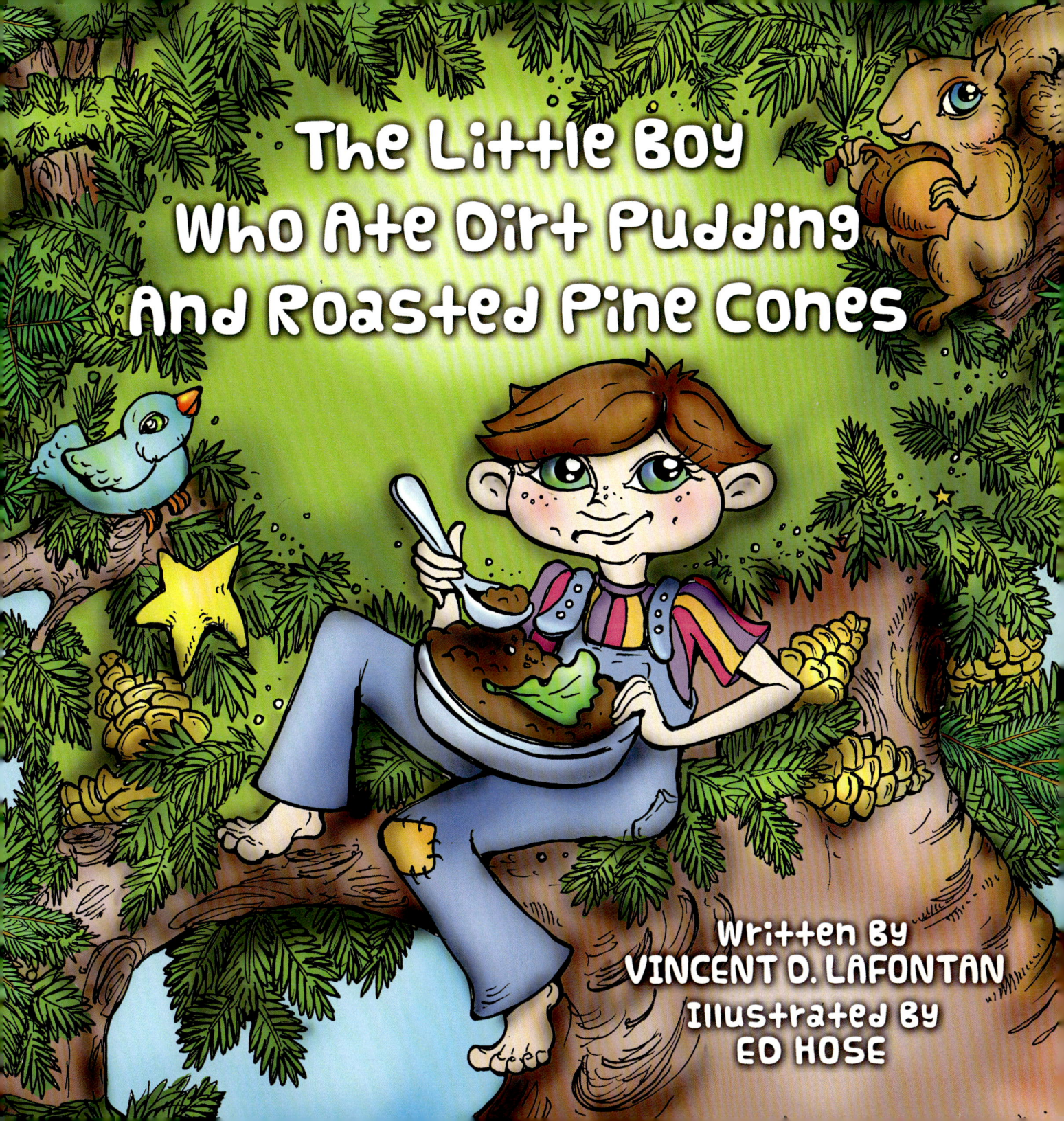

The Little Boy Who Ate Dirt Pudding and Roasted Pine Cones

Written by Vincent D. LaFontan

Illustrated by ED Hose

Book Design by Terry Wilson

©Copyright 2013 by Vincent D. LaFontan. All rights reserved.

No part of this book may be reproduced or copied in any form.

ISBN 978-0-9890447-0-7

Mountain Books

Kent, CT 06757 USA

www.kentmountainbooks.com

*To Olivia and Abigail,
my little squirrels!*

In a little wooden house, way outside of town, lived a little boy. He had a wonderful life. He was cared for by his parents who loved him very much and he had everything he needed.

He did not, however, have everything he wanted.

Each day the little boy would ask his mother what is for dinner. "Dirt pudding and roasted pine cones," his mother would say, "you know they are delicious and fill up our bellies before bed. This way you will grow-up to be a strong little man!"

"I wish I could have something different instead!" the little boy would reply. Then his mother would just simply pat him on the head.

One day while walking home from school, the little boy passed a big tent that read: "Come one, come all, to the greatest show outside of town. The Circus, the Circus, fun for all ages!"

How could the little boy resist! He went right in and was greeted by a ballerina bear riding a tricycle and a tightrope walker performing overhead.

But even more exciting to the little boy was the smell in the air…….

He smelled something delicious! So he waited until the end of the show and he went up to the Ringmaster. "What is that wonderful smell?" asked the little boy.

The Ringmaster laughed. "Come with me young man," he replied, as he led the little boy behind the curtain at the back of the tent.

Wow! The circus performers were all there--laughing and singing and eating away!

They had popcorn and cotton candy, pretzels and peanuts, licorice sticks and buckets of ice cream.

Right there at that moment, the little boy made up his mind, no more dirt pudding and no more roasted pine cones—its candy and popcorn for me, he thought.

He would join the circus and have everything he ever wanted!

At first this was an exciting new life, the circus would move from one town to the next and the little boy would help set up and take down the big tent.

Then after every night's show he would eat to his heart's content all the things he had dreamed about but never had with his parents in the little wooden house.

But as the seasons went by the time on the road started to be grey.

One night the little boy didn't even join the circus performers for their sweet dinner after the show; instead he just went to bed and dreamed of a little roasted pine cone to warm his belly.

Before he knew it a year had gone by and the little boy's circus kept going from town to town.

One foggy morning, as the circus wagons were driving along, the little boy peeked out of his wagon and recognized a field and a stream.

He knew right away they were heading into his hometown and he became excited to see his parents again!

After the show that night he went to the Ringmaster and asked to go see his parents. "You are in the circus now, we don't have time for such things," said the Ringmaster. This made the little boy very sad and he went into his tent to cry.

When darkness fell and all the Circus performers went to sleep, the little boy decided to escape.

He left the circus and started walking on the road towards his home. Quickly it became very dark and the little boy had trouble finding his way.

Soon he was lost and became so scared that he just stopped and sat at the base of a big tree and cried.

Then, when everything was so dark and terrible, his hand felt something on the ground next to him.

It was long and rough and pricked a little when he picked it up. But as soon as he smelled it, he knew what it was, a delicious little pine cone, the kind his father would gather for his mother to roast.

These memories gave him the courage to stand-up and keep walking, which he did for a minute until he started to run, all the way to the little wooden house way outside of town.

When he got to the house he knocked on the door and his mother and father greeted him with kisses and hugs and through their tears they said "little boy, little boy, we have missed you so. We searched everywhere and didn't know where did you go!" The little boy told them his story and promised never to do it again.

"You must be so hungry from all your travels tonight," asked his mother. "I know just the thing," said his father, "we'll make you some dirt pudding and roasted pine cones so you can feel at home again."

"That's just what I need and just what I wanted, too!" the little boy said with a big smile.

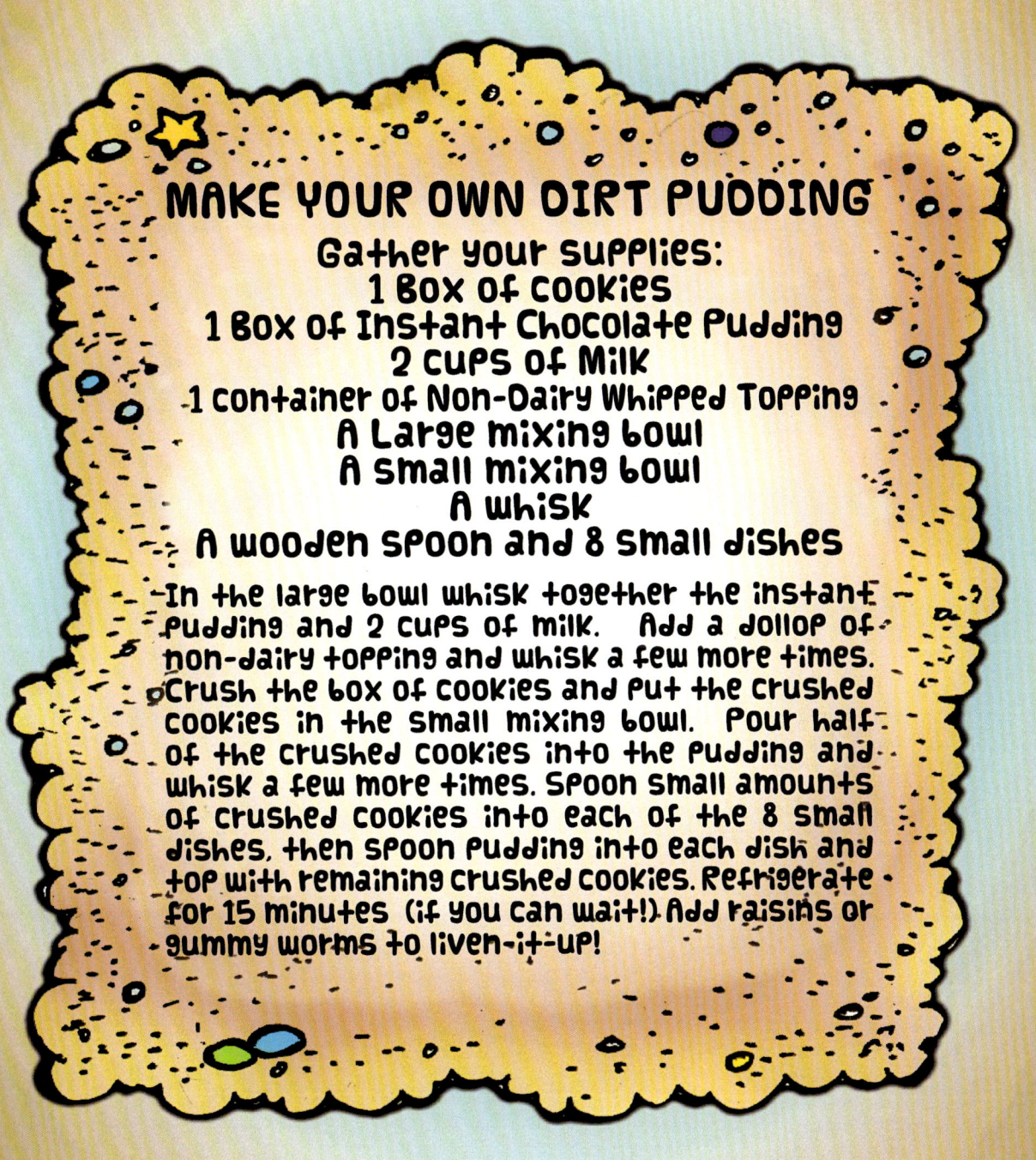

MAKE YOUR OWN DIRT PUDDING

Gather your supplies:
1 Box of Cookies
1 Box of Instant Chocolate Pudding
2 Cups of Milk
1 Container of Non-Dairy Whipped Topping
A Large mixing bowl
A Small mixing bowl
A Whisk
A wooden spoon and 8 small dishes

In the large bowl whisk together the instant pudding and 2 cups of milk. Add a dollop of non-dairy topping and whisk a few more times. Crush the box of cookies and put the crushed cookies in the small mixing bowl. Pour half of the crushed cookies into the pudding and whisk a few more times. Spoon small amounts of crushed cookies into each of the 8 small dishes, then spoon pudding into each dish and top with remaining crushed cookies. Refrigerate for 15 minutes (if you can wait!) Add raisins or gummy worms to liven-it-up!

Vincent D. Lafontan has worked with children and youth for many years and is a nationally recognized leader in the field of After School and Out of School time programming. He is a lifelong resident of Kent, Connecticut where he lives on Mountain View Farm with his wife, Maria and daughters Olivia and Abigail. Vince has shared his love of storytelling with thousands of children and families and was recognized for his popular "History of Maple Syrup Making, an American Tale" presentation as well as many other hands-on programs for children focused on nature, agriculture and history. Vince stresses the importance of allowing children time to play and use their imaginations every day — and hopes his tales paint a safe, fun place to enjoy.

Photo by Sarah Deshaw

ED Hose lives on the coast of Georgia with her two young sons and incredibly old dog. She works as a freelance illustrator. Her passion for whimsical details makes her style easily recognizable. ED's murals, portraits, books and fine art can be seen across the country. When not creating art, she can be found in the kitchen creating a mess.
www.edhose.com